D0745634

WITHDRAWN

First Facts®

Water in Our World

The Water Cycle at Work

by Rebecca Olien

CAPSTONE PRESS
a capstone imprint

First Facts are published by Capstone Press,
1710 Roe Crest Drive, North Mankato, Minnesota 56003
www.capstonepub.com

Copyright © 2016 by Capstone Press, a Capstone imprint. All rights reserved. No part of this publication may be reproduced in whole or in part, or stored in a retrieval system, or transmitted in any form or by any means, electronic, mechanical, photocopying, recording, or otherwise, without written permission of the publisher.

Library of Congress Cataloging-in-Publication Data
Olien, Rebecca, author.
  The water cycle at work / by Rebecca Olien. — [New edition]
      pages cm. — (First facts. Water in our world)
  Summary: "Explains the stages of the water cycle and how the water cycle impacts Earth's water supply"— Provided by publisher.
  Audience: Ages 7-9.
  Audience: K to grade 3.
  Includes bibliographical references and index.
  ISBN 978-1-4914-8273-5 (library binding)
  ISBN 978-1-4914-8280-3 (paperback)
  ISBN 978-1-4914-8284-1 (eBook PDF)
  1. Water—Juvenile literature. 2. Hydrologic cycle—Juvenile literature. I. Title.
  GB662.3.O578 2016
  551.48—dc23
                              2015026111

Editorial Credits
Abby Colich, editor; Kyle Grenz, designer; Wanda Winch, media researcher; Laura Manthe, production specialist

Photo Credits
Capstone, 7; Corbis: Joe McBride, 11; Shutterstock: DrimaFilm, 1, Ecelop, waves design, grublee, 8, JaroPienza, 18, Julia Kurm, 13, Kotenko Oleksandr, cover, Nadalina, 5, papa studio, 14-15, paula french, 20, Radu Bercan, 16-17, tachyglossus, splash design

Printed and bound in China.
007480RRDS16

Table of Contents

Water Covers the Earth

From space, Earth looks like a round blue ball with swirls of white. The blue color is water. The white is clouds. Water covers 70 percent of Earth. Water moves and changes as part of the water *cycle*.

cycle—something that happens over and over again

Fact!

Earth is sometimes called "the Blue Planet."

The Water Cycle

Water changes as it moves through the water cycle. Water *evaporates* as it changes from a liquid into a gas, or *vapor*. Water vapor *condenses* to form clouds. *Precipitation* falls from clouds as rain or snow. The sun's heat turns liquid water back into gas. Then the water cycle begins again. Let's take a closer look at each part of this cycle.

evaporate—the action of a liquid changing into a gas
vapor—a substance in gas form
condense—to change from a gas into a liquid
precipitation—water that falls from the sky as rain, sleet, snow, or hail

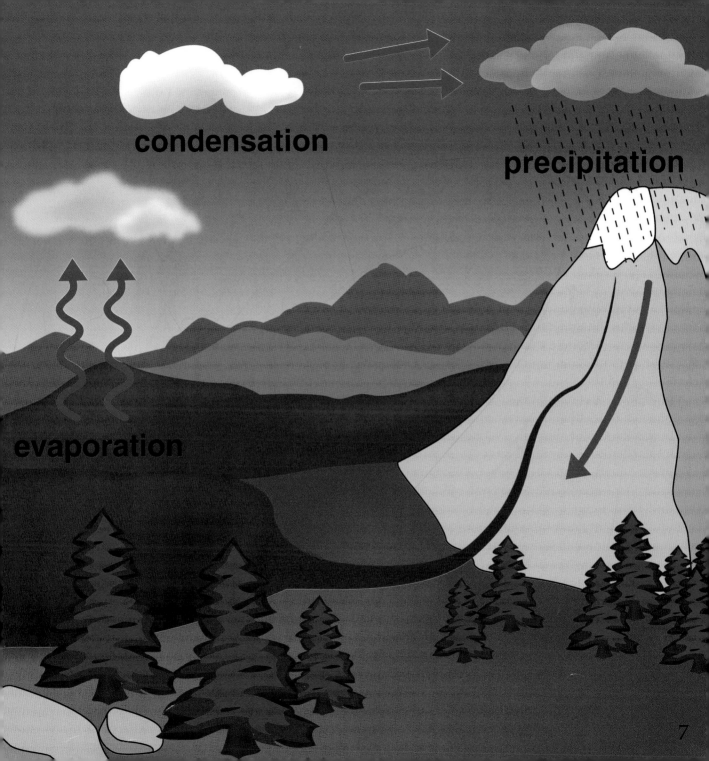

condensation

precipitation

evaporation

Evaporation

One way the water cycle can begin is with evaporation. The sun's heat makes water change from a liquid to vapor during evaporation.

People can't see water vapor. Vapor can only be seen when it is mixed with water drops. You can see vapor as steam coming from a cup of hot cocoa.

Humidity

Humidity is the amount of water vapor in the air. Humidity changes with the temperature. Warm air holds more water vapor than cold air. People feel warmer on humid days because sweat does not evaporate quickly.

Fact!

Your hair is slightly longer on humid days. Humidity can make a strand of hair up to 3 percent longer.

humidity—the measure of the moisture in the air

Condensation

A very humid day can lead to a lot of water condensation. Condensation takes place when water changes from vapor back into liquid. Vapor turns into droplets as air cools. You can see condensation as dewdrops on leaves. Condensation also forms on the outside of a glass of cold water.

Clouds

Clouds are another form of condensation. Vapor becomes water droplets around specks of dust in the sky. These droplets stick together to make clouds.

Clouds grow heavy with water as condensation takes place. Dark clouds are filled with water. Rain is on the way.

Fact!

Fog is a cloud that's close to the ground.

15

Precipitation

Precipitation is the final part of the water cycle. Water falls from clouds as precipitation. Rain falls when clouds fill with water. Frozen water falls as snow, *sleet,* or *hail.*

Precipitation *replenishes* water on Earth. Rain *seeps* into the soil to restore water in the ground. Rain and snow fall in rivers, lakes, and oceans.

sleet—rain that freezes as it's falling and hits the ground as frozen pellets of ice
hail—small balls of ice that form in thunderstorm clouds
replenish—to make full again
seep—to flow or trickle slowly

Fact!

Freezing rain is rain that freezes after it hits the ground.

An Endless Cycle

Saving water helps make sure all living things have the freshwater they need. People, plants, and animals share the same freshwater. Everyone must work together to save water and keep it clean.

Amazing But True!

The water people drink today is the same water dinosaurs drank millions of years ago. Earth's water is about 3 billion years old. The water cycle keeps water on the planet. In the future, people, plants, and animals will also use this same water.

Hands On: Water Cycle Cups

Water is the only substance found in nature as a liquid, a solid, and a gas. Try this activity to see how water changes into its different forms as part of the water cycle.

What You Need

- 2 clear plastic cups
- hot tap water
- ice cube

What You Do

1. Fill one plastic cup with about 1 inch (2.5 centimeters) of hot tap water.
2. Quickly place the second cup upside down on top of the first cup. Make sure that the rims of the cups are connected.
3. Place an ice cube on top of the stacked cups.
4. Look for the different states of water in the water cycle. Water vapor rises into the top cup. The ice cools the air so tiny droplets form. As the drops get bigger, they fall back into the cup like rain.

Glossary

condense (kuhn-DENSS)—to change from a gas into a liquid

cycle (SYE-kuhl)—something that happens over and over again

evaporate (e-VAP-uh-rate)—the action of a liquid changing into a gas

hail (HAYL)—small balls of ice that form in thunderstorm clouds

humidity (hyoo-MIH-du-tee)—the measure of the moisture in the air

precipitation (pri-sip-i-TAY-shuhn)—water that falls from the sky as rain, sleet, snow, or hail

replenish (ri-PLEN-ish)—to make full again

seep (SEEP)—to flow or trickle slowly

sleet (SLEET)—rain that freezes as it's falling and hits the ground as frozen pellets of ice

vapor (VAY-pur)—a substance in gas form

Read More

Dakers, Diane. *Earth's Water Cycle*. Earth's Cycles in Action. New York: Crabtree Publishing, 2015.

Duke, Shirley Smith. *Step-by-Step Experiments with the Water Cycle*. Mankato, Minn.: The Child's World, 2012.

Maloof, Torrey. *Water Cycle*. Science Readers. Huntington Beach, Calif.: Teacher Created Materials, 2015.

Internet Sites

FactHound offers a safe, fun way to find Internet sites related to this book. All of the sites on FactHound have been researched by our staff.

Here's all you do:

Visit *www.facthound.com*

Type in this code: 9781491482735

Check out projects, games and lots more at
www.capstonekids.com

Critical Thinking Using the Common Core

1. Name and describe one part of the water cycle. (Key Idea and Details)
2. Reread pages 12 and 14 and study the photos. How are the two forms of condensation alike? How are they different? (Integration of Knowledge and Ideas)
3. Page 16 says that precipitation replenishes water to the Earth. Why is this a necessary part of the water cycle? (Craft and Structure)

Index